IMAGES
of America

FIRST TROOP PHILADELPHIA CITY CAVALRY

ARMORY OF FIRST CITY TROOPS,
PHILADELPHIA, PA.

This postcard shows the troop's current armory as it looked shortly after its completion in April 1901. Although the neighborhood around the armory has developed considerably, the armory has undergone relatively few external renovations in over a century.

On the cover: The First City Troop has provided a military escort in numerous parades since 1775. In 1915, the Liberty Bell left Philadelphia for the last time, during which time it formed part of an exhibit for the Pan-American Exposition in San Francisco. Here Capt. J. Franklin McFadden leads the troop as it escorts the bell past Independence Hall. (Museum of the First Troop Philadelphia City Cavalry.)

IMAGES
of America

FIRST TROOP PHILADELPHIA CITY CAVALRY

Joseph Seymour

ARCADIA
PUBLISHING

Published by Arcadia Publishing
Charleston SC, Chicago IL, Portsmouth NH, San Francisco CA

Printed in the United States of America

Library of Congress Catalog Card Number: 2007935811

For all general information contact Arcadia Publishing at:
Telephone 843-853-2070
Fax 843-853-0044
E-mail sales@arcadiapublishing.com
For customer service and orders:
Toll-Free 1-888-313-2665

Visit us on the Internet at www.arcadiapublishing.com

*To the officers and gentlemen of the First City Troop past and present,
for your ongoing service to the nation and commitment to
maintaining this fine tradition. This is your work.*

CONTENTS

Acknowledgments   6

Introduction   7

1.   Service to the Nation   9

2.   Armories and Artifacts   59

3.   Celebrating City Life   71

4.   A Living Legacy   95

Troop Captains   127

ACKNOWLEDGMENTS

Since the First Troop Philadelphia City Cavalry's founding in 1774, hundreds of troopers have contributed archives, artifacts, and images to its collection. It would be impossible to name all the individuals who contributed to this project, but the efforts of a few individuals bear mention. Foremost I would like to thank Dennis J. Boylan for his unswerving support of this project. I would also like to thank Capt. Anselm T. W. Richards of the First City Troop. To Norris V. Claytor, John C. Devereux, Jack Tomarchio, Craig Nannos, Steve Morgan, and Eric Reinholt goes my gratitude for their always constant and often intangible support and advice. I am grateful to John Bansemer, who provided advice and many of the initial scans. Thanks also go to Erin Vosgien at Arcadia Publishing for giving the troop this opportunity to tell its story to a wider audience. The staff of Techlab in Baltimore, Maryland, processed the final scans and provided 11th-hour support for this project. Finally I would like to extend my heartfelt thanks to Johanna Wharton for transcribing parts of the text, proofreading, and just plain putting up with this project for so long. All images that appear in this work were provided by the Museum of the First Troop Philadelphia City Cavalry.

INTRODUCTION

Organized on November 17, 1774, as the Light Horse of the City of Philadelphia, the First Troop Philadelphia City Cavalry is the oldest mounted unit in the United States Army and one of the oldest units in the Army National Guard. On that day, 28 Philadelphians, concerned for the security of their city and the safety of their ideals, elected Abraham Markoe captain and pledged to train for the defense of their city.

Members of the Philadelphia Light Horse envisioned a reconnaissance role for their new unit. But as their home was the capital city of the Revolution, higher duties soon called. The troop embarked on the first of many calls to active service on June 20, 1775, when it escorted Gen. George Washington to New York City. Following this mission, the troop returned home to attend to both official and private affairs.

It was at about this time that King Christian VII of Denmark issued his edict forbidding his subjects to bear arms against King George III of England on pain of having their property confiscated. Markoe owned extensive tracts of land on the island of St. Croix, lands that supported a considerable income. The troop, understanding that Markoe's contribution to the patriot cause exceeded his commission as captain of the Light Horse, allowed Markoe to resign.

Although Markoe's tenure was short, its impact was far-reaching. During the Revolutionary War, troopers made conspicuous contributions in and out of uniform. Capt. Samuel Morris, who succeeded Markoe, sat on the Philadelphia Committee of Safety. Troopers outfitted private warships and contributed to financier Robert Morris's Bank of North America, rescuing the United States from financial ruin. Lt. John Dunlap printed the first copies of the Declaration of Independence.

In addition to these contributions, the troop was still a fighting unit. Mustered into Continental service on July 30, 1776, to defend New Jersey, the troop suffered its first casualty in August when trooper George Fullerton was accidentally killed. In December, troopers rode to the aid of the retreating Continental army in New Jersey and swam their horses across the icy Delaware River on Christmas night. The troop fought the next day at the Battle of Trenton and carried the colors of the captured Hessian regiments to Congress. A week later, the troop again showed its mettle at the Battle of Princeton, when, in defense of a retreating company of Philadelphia artillery, the troop held a bridge against a detachment of British cavalry. For these actions, Washington wrote the troop a special letter of thanks.

Mustered into federal service on September 10, 1794, the troop helped quell the Whiskey Rebellion in western Pennsylvania and shortly thereafter began calling itself the First Troop Philadelphia City Cavalry, the name it bears today. The troop defended Philadelphia during the War of 1812, contributed officers and men for the United States Army during the war with

Mexico, and helped quell civil disturbances in the decades leading up to the Civil War. In 1853, the troop built its first armory. The troop currently occupies its third armory.

In May 1861, Pres. Abraham Lincoln called for 75,000 volunteers for three months' service. The troop fought at Falling Water, an early action in the Civil War, before mustering out in August. Just as Markoe had done during the Revolutionary War, many troopers understood that they could do a lot more to preserve the Union than sit in a saddle and wield a saber, while other troopers volunteered to do just that. So while older members of the First City Troop remained in state service with the Pennsylvania Militia, younger troopers furnished cadre for the 6th Regiment, Pennsylvania Volunteer Cavalry. Organized on June 18, 1863, at Philadelphia, and better known as Rush's Lancers, the 6th Pennsylvania amassed a commendable service record during the war. The older members who stayed behind were no shirkers: during the summer of 1863, the First City Troop served with distinction at Wrightsville and Gettysburg.

Following the war, veterans of both organizations reunited at their armory in Philadelphia, and by the troop's centennial in November 1874, the organization was as strong as ever.

The troop continued to serve the city and commonwealth, quelling riots and keeping the peace during the Gilded Age. When the nation called following the destruction of the USS *Maine* at Havana, Cuba, the troop was ready to ride. Mustered into federal service on May 7, 1898, the troop served in Puerto Rico until the Spanish surrender. The next period of active service for the troop came in July 1916, after depredations of Francisco "Pancho" Villa took the United States and Mexico to the brink of war. The Mexican border service also inaugurated an annual equestrian competition known as the Border Plate. This classic showcases troopers' equestrian abilities.

Troopers laid aside thoughts of such pleasantries on July 23, 1917, as they left their homes and loved ones to fight in World War I. With little room for horses in the trenches of the western front, the troop fought in France as the 103rd Trench Mortar Battery.

Following the war, the troop reorganized first as a line troop of horse cavalry and later as Headquarters Troop, 52nd Cavalry Brigade, an element of the 22nd Cavalry Division, while keeping its traditional designation and honors intact.

Inducted into federal service on February 17, 1941, at Philadelphia, the troop departed Philadelphia to train for war. On April 9, 1942, a sad day in the memories of those who were present, troopers traded their mounts for jeeps and motorcycles. While the troop continues to maintain its equestrian tradition, it has been a mechanized cavalry troop since World War II. Approximately 50 percent of the troop's enlisted personnel were commissioned as officers during World War II. Troop A continued in federal service. The troop suffered several casualties before the end of hostilities on May 8, 1945.

The service of Troop A tells only part of the story. During the war, troopers served in every branch of the military. Most served in the army. Charles S. Cheston rose to brigadier general. One trooper even became a war correspondent. In total, 271 troopers saw service in World War II. Ten lost their lives. So while Troop A saw little active campaigning during the war, members of the First City Troop were very active indeed.

Reorganized and redesignated on December 1, 1948, as the 28th Reconnaissance Troop, and known as Troop A, 1st Squadron, 104th Cavalry, since April 1, 1975, troopers wear the red keystone patch of the 28th Infantry Division. Ordered into active federal service on May 31, 2002, at Philadelphia, the First City Troop spent seven months in Bosnia and Herzegovina enforcing the Dayton Peace Accords. Troopers currently fight in the Global War on Terrorism in Iraq, Afghanistan, and other parts of the Middle East.

Troopers of today are very much like their Revolutionary War predecessors, citizens concerned for the defense of their city, their liberty, and their nation. Although the troop enjoys pomp, circumstance, and many fun-filled events, its members are all acutely aware of the many sacrifices of their forebears and the continuing legacy of the nation's oldest mounted unit.

One

SERVICE TO THE NATION

John Wagner Jr. served the troop from 1889 until 1901, and again from 1918 to 1930, rising from the rank of private to cornet, the most junior officer rank. Such long periods of service are not uncommon in the troop. John Wagner Jr. stands here with the troop guidon in Puerto Rico during the Spanish-American War. The guidon, still in the troop's possession, is of red and white cloth, the cavalry colors, and reads, "First Troop PCC."

The captain of the Philadelphia Light Horse during the Battles of Trenton, Princeton, and Brandywine, Samuel Morris was born on June 24, 1734, and raised in the Society of Friends. An avid sportsman, "Quaker Sam" was a member of the Schuylkill Company of Fort St. David, governor of the colony (later state) in Schuylkill, and president of the Gloucester Hunt Club. Morris was an early supporter of resistance to Great Britain's policies. Despite his Quaker beliefs, Morris joined the troop when it organized on November 17, 1774, and held prominent positions in the committee of safety. Morris led the troop when it crossed the Delaware River with Gen. George Washington on December 25, 1776. Morris and the Philadelphia Light Horse fought and won a rearguard action against a British cavalry detachment at the Stony Brook Bridge at the conclusion of the Battle of Princeton. This image is from a portrait donated by Effingham B. Morris.

Samuel Miles was already an experienced soldier before joining the ranks of the troop on October 6, 1781. Miles had commanded the Pennsylvania State Rifle Regiment in 1776. He left the active command of the troop in 1790 to become mayor of Philadelphia. The town of Milesburg, in Centre County, is named for Miles.

Another older soldier who counted years of military service before becoming troop captain, Christian Febiger served with distinction as an officer in both the Danish army and the Continental army during the Revolutionary War. A veteran of the Battles of Bunker Hill, Quebec, Brandywine, Monmouth, Stony Point, and Yorktown, Febiger was also an experienced statesman who served in the Virginia legislature and as treasurer of the Commonwealth of Pennsylvania.

Charles Ross joined the troop in 1794 and served as a private when the troop rode into western Pennsylvania to quell the Whiskey Rebellion that year. In 1811, the troop elected Ross as its captain. Ross led the troop when it mustered for service during the War of 1812, and he continued as captain following the war. A successful merchant in the China trade, Ross died as a result of a shipborne disease in 1817. His funeral was one of the largest in the city of Philadelphia. He was buried with full military honors in the cemetery of the Fourth Presbyterian Church in Philadelphia. His tombstone, shown here, topped with a bronze sculpture of crossed sabers and troop helmet, has fallen victim to vandalism in recent years.

Robert Wharton and 13 troopers organized the volunteer troop of light dragoons in the summer of 1798. The dragoons escorted prisoners captured at sea during the Quasi-War with France. Following this duty, the light dragoons disbanded, and its members returned to the ranks of the parent organization. Wharton later served as captain of the First City Troop, mayor of Philadelphia, colonel of the regiment of city cavalry, and brigadier general of the 1st Brigade, 1st Division, of the Pennsylvania Militia.

In May 1861, after mustering into federal service, the troop drilled every day at Fairmount Park, Point Breeze Park, or on South Broad Street and assembled every night at its armory, in the third story of the building at the southwest corner of Twelfth and Chestnut Streets. The troop decided against wearing its own uniform, and so, on May 23, 1861, the troop marched to the Schuylkill Armory at nearby Gray's Ferry and drew a regulation U.S. Cavalry uniform, each man paying for his own kit, and marched back to the armory carrying the bundles. Edwin A. Lewis is shown here in early 1861 wearing his cavalry uniform.

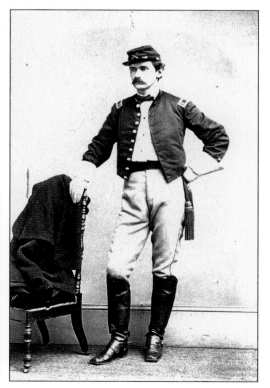

At the end of three months' service, the troop returned home to Philadelphia. Many troopers thereafter helped organize the 6th Regiment, Pennsylvania Volunteer Cavalry, known also as Rush's Lancers. The 6th Pennsylvania's nickname came from the fact that the regiment, organized in 1861 by Richard H. Rush, carried lances into battle. Rudulph Ellis, who joined the troop on May 6, 1861, joined the 6th Pennsylvania in 1862. Wounded that year at Beverly Ford, Ellis rose to the rank of captain by war's end. The insignia on his shoulder and sash identify him as an adjutant in this famous regiment. Adjutants were officers responsible for administrative duties within regiments.

William A. Borthwick is shown here in the uniform of a lieutenant of cavalry. The crossed sabers on his hat represent the cavalry branch, and the No. 6 identifies him as a member of the 6th Pennsylvania Cavalry. Borthwick survived the war and later traveled to Texas, where he died in 1872.

Gilbert Newhall is shown here in the troop's service dress. The white belt over his left shoulder holds a saber that is not visible in the portrait. Newhall joined the troop in September 1863 and served throughout the Civil War. Following the war, Newhall left the army and the troop for good.

Trooper Joseph Penrose Ash enlisted in the First City Troop at the age of 17 on June 6, 1859. Following news of the surrender of Fort Sumter in 1861, Ash reported to Washington, D.C., where he was commissioned as a second lieutenant in the 5th U.S. Cavalry. Ash received three saber cuts at the Battle of Warrenton in 1862 and was promoted to major for his valorous conduct in that action. A distinguished soldier noted for his brave conduct in battle, Ash was killed at the head of his troops near Alsop's Farm during the Battle of Spotsylvania, on May 8, 1864, and promoted posthumously to the rank of lieutenant colonel.

Some troopers also helped organize the 2nd Pennsylvania Cavalry. Shown here is Col. R. Butler Price. Price served with the troop for slightly less than six months in 1826, before rejoining the organization in 1830. Price served with the troop as a private when the troop mustered into state service to put down an armed mob at the state capitol in Harrisburg in 1839 and likely served during the Kensington Riots that rocked the city of Philadelphia in 1844 during a series of civil disturbances known as the "Buckshot Wars," so named because the involved troops were ordered to load their muskets with buckshot to disperse unruly mobs. In 1861, Price helped organize the 2nd Pennsylvania Cavalry. On September 7, 1861, he became the regiment's colonel. He served in the general headquarters of the Army of the Potomac at the Battle of Gettysburg and rose to the rank of brigadier general by the end of the war. Price died on July 15, 1876.

Two brothers who served both the troop and the 2nd Pennsylvania Cavalry are shown here. At right is Charles F. Taggart. Charles joined the troop in 1857. In 1861, he left the troop to accept a commission as a major in the 2nd Pennsylvania. Wounded in battle on October 22, 1863, Charles died two days later at Warrenton, Virginia. His brother William H. Taggart was more fortunate. William joined the troop in 1859 and entered federal service in 1861, being commissioned as a surgeon in the same regiment as his brother. William served for a year, from 1861 to 1862, and returned to the troop after the war. He died on September 20, 1899.

During the 19th century, mounted drill took place in any nearby open space that was available. These photographs, taken in the 1880s and 1890s, give some idea of what a troop drill might have looked like between the Civil War and the Spanish-American War. At this time, the Pennsylvania Militia took lessons learned from the Civil War to foster a greater state of military preparedness. In the forefront of this trend, the troop regularly drilled at its armory and on any available open space in and around Philadelphia. The most common drill spaces were at nearby Fairmount Park, Point Breeze Park, or on farms near the Philadelphia suburb of Norristown. The photograph above shows the troop divided into two subdivisions known as platoons. The photograph below, probably taken during the 1890 annual encampment at Norristown, shows troopers formed in line with sabers drawn, such as they might have done in preparation for a saber charge.

Shown here are two troopers at an annual summer encampment. They wear the regulation five-button tunic and khaki slouch hat authorized in the late 1880s. The trooper on the right holds a model 1873 Springfield carbine, the standard-issue cavalry weapon, along with the saber, one of which is visible just behind the central tent post. During summer encampments, National Guard troops were evaluated in all aspects of training, organization, and equipment.

The troop has always prided itself in marksmanship and has fielded several winning rifle and pistol teams. At the August 24, 1896, match held at Mount Gretna, with the .45-caliber Springfield carbines shown here, the troop finished first among the three troops of the Pennsylvania Cavalry. The Sheridan Troop of Tyrone finished second, and the Governor's Troop of Harrisburg finished third.

In 1897, miners in the anthracite coal regions of northeastern Pennsylvania demanded better wages and improved working conditions. Confrontations between coal miners and sheriffs' deputies grew increasingly violent. In Luzerne County on September 10 of that year, 500 men attacked a sheriff and his deputies, who opened fire and killed and wounded dozens of miners. As the situation grew more dangerous, the governor ordered an entire National Guard brigade, including the troop, to Hazleton on September 11. The troop received its orders at 11:30 in the morning. Four hours later, it marched out of its armory and boarded the Baltimore and Ohio Railroad line a block away. Live ammunition was issued on the train, which arrived at Hazleton at 9:30 that night. By the next morning, a city of tents stood in an open field outside Hazleton. The troop sent daily patrols to nearby towns. The photograph below shows one such patrol being inspected before departing. The troop remained on this duty until September 28 before being dismissed.

Congress declared war on Spain on April 5, 1898. On April 28, the troop assembled at the armory and entered federal service under the command of Capt. John C. Groome Sr. Following training at Mount Gretna and Camp Alger, the troop entrained for Newport News, Virginia, where it boarded the transport *Massachusetts* bound for Puerto Rico. Groome stands behind the troop guidon with his officers. To his right are Lt. Edward Browning and J. Franklin McFadden at far left.

The transport *Massachusetts* ran aground as it sailed into the harbor in Puerto Rico. Following a tense evening, the troop was ordered ashore on August 3, 1898. It is shown here unloading horses from a barge known as a lighter. Note the mixture of service blue uniforms and the newer, more advanced khaki uniforms.

Men and horses suffered terribly in the tropical heat of Puerto Rico. The troop was nonetheless successful in keeping its mounts healthy. This picket line shows a row of gaunt, but healthy and well-groomed horses. In the name of uniformity, the army habitually issued mounts of a single color to each cavalry troop. While at Mount Gretna, the troop received its allotment of gray horses. The mixed color of mounts in this picket line is indicative of the high rate of attrition to mounts in the tropical climate.

On August 12, the troop saddled up and rode to Guayama to join a battery of the Pennsylvania Volunteer Field Artillery. Although reports of small parties of armed Spaniards proved untrue, the advance through canebrakes and heavy underbrush was nonetheless slow and dangerous. The extreme heat took its toll on men and horses, leading Capt. John C. Groome Sr. to call for frequent dismounts. Here the troop marches toward Cayey past fields of sugarcane.

The troop spotted fresh entrenchments on the approach to Cayey. There headquarters ordered Groome to attack the Spanish positions with artillery support. The troop was ordered to mount and move out toward Guayama. Each trooper wore a mix of blue wool uniforms and the newer khaki uniforms. Before the attack could commence, a lieutenant from the general staff arrived with news of the cease-fire. The Spanish-American War had ended.

This photograph shows the crowded conditions aboard the transports that brought the troop and its horses to and from Puerto Rico. In all, approximately 1,200 soldiers and nearly as many horses crammed aboard the transport ship *Massachusetts*. The heat and stench from the horses kept most men on deck. This photograph was probably taken aboard the transport *Mississippi* during the return voyage.

The troop boarded the transport *Mississippi* on August 23, 1898, and reached New York City on September 10. Here are two views of life aboard a troop transport. The view above shows a soldier inspecting one of many canvas vents rigged by the crew of the transport ships to circulate fresh air into the hold below. In the view below, six troopers find limited shade underneath one of the transport's lifeboats. One trooper reads a letter from home while another trooper, with his back to the camera, has found a makeshift deck chair in the form of the lifeboat's cradle. He braves the heat in a blue army tunic.

Soldiers lay sprawled out on the decks of the transport ship. While many accounts describe troopers sleeping on bales of hay on deck, some have taken the hammocks they were provided with and have suspended them from the ship's rigging.

Troop officers dine in Puerto Rico. The officers were better provided than the enlisted men; in addition to their tents, they were provided with this additional mess fly, a tent without walls that could be used for reading maps as well as dining. Relatively speaking, these officers are uniformly dressed, suggesting that this photograph was taken after the cease-fire.

Another view of troop officers in the field shows Capt. John C. Groome Sr. (left) conferring with his lieutenants and an unidentified individual. A horse bridle hangs from a nearby fence post.

An army wagon, known as an escort wagon, is here shown during a brief halt in Puerto Rico. Escort wagons were commonly used for a variety of purposes. The troop wore a mixture of uniforms, but civilian hats were strictly proscribed. The individual at left wearing the civilian hat also carries a pair of binoculars and may be a war correspondent.

An army escort wagon is here shown mired down in the mud, somewhere in Puerto Rico. Mules were a new experience for many troopers familiar with horses. The idiosyncrasies of mules, especially their tendency to bray at one another in the morning, won them very little sympathy from the horse soldiers.

The troop established an outpost called Camp Esperanza in the vicinity Cayey in Puerto Rico. A beach about three miles from camp provided a welcome respite from the tropical heat. Here troopers enjoy a relaxing swim with their mounts. Many troopers became very proficient in the sport of swimming their horses.

The journey to and from Puerto Rico was filled with hours of boredom. The sight of land was a welcome one, whether it was the mountains of Puerto Rico (shown here) or Sandy Hook, which was the first landfall for the troop on its voyage home from war.

The transport *Mississippi* made landfall at the rail terminal in Jersey City on the return from Puerto Rico. There were no bridges or tunnels between Manhattan and New Jersey in 1898; passengers traveling between New Jersey and New York took a ferry from the railhead at Jersey City to New York. As this rail line connected directly to Philadelphia, the troopers were welcomed by well-wishers from home.

On September 10, 1898, troopers returning from Puerto Rico steamed into New York Harbor. Through the mist, troopers made out the notes of a bugle playing the familiar "First City Troop March and Two-Step." Ellis Pugh, the troop trumpeter medically barred from serving with the troop in Puerto Rico, had come all the way from Philadelphia to welcome his comrades home.

Following the Spanish-American War, the troop returned to its routine of weekly drills and annual summer encampments. This photograph shows the troop on the rifle range at Mount Gretna early in the 20th century. The troopers fire the Model 1903 Springfield rifle under the watchful gaze of a senior army advisor, seated at right. The signs marked 2 and 3 are firing positions. The building in the background is a range house, which was moved from Mount Gretna to Indiantown Gap in the late 20th century. While in summer encampment, the soldiers slept in tents, visible in the background.

Two troopers standing in camp about 1916 wear the regulation uniform approved for cavalry and full field gear, including the Model 1911 .45-caliber pistol that had replaced the saber as the trooper's principal weapon by this time. The soldier in the rear wears gauntlets.

On June 22, 1916, the troop mustered into federal service in response to tensions caused as a result of raids by Francisco "Pancho" Villa. Following several weeks of training at Mount Gretna, the troop traveled by train to Fort Bliss, Texas, near El Paso. The troop is shown here in formation shortly after its arrival. Many of the troopers wear special dust goggles on their campaign hats. The troop marched two miles from the railhead to its temporary home of Camp Stewart.

Capt. J. Franklin McFadden, shown here during the Mexican border service, was an accomplished equestrian in civilian life. This photograph was probably taken during a period of light duty, as he is shown without the extensive field equipment that cavalry soldiers usually carried on patrol. He wears the regulation cavalry uniform, with captain's rank on his collar and the insignia of the 1st Pennsylvania Cavalry on his chevraque, the padded cloth under his 1904 McClellan saddle.

On the Mexican border, troopers trained hard under some of the most severe weather conditions in the Southwest. This photograph was most likely taken during the march to the Dona Anna rifle range, as the troopers have only their saddles and rifles. The trooper at left prudently carries his Model 1903 Springfield rifle in his saddle scabbard to protect it from the elements.

This trooper was probably photographed in 1916 at Mount Gretna as the troop prepared for Mexican border service. While at Mount Gretna, troopers were subjected to grueling training such as crawling through high grass—a relatively new tactic in 1916. This trooper wears a four-dent Montana peak campaign hat and shoulders a Model 1903 Springfield rifle.

Troopers set up a mess tent at Camp Stewart on the Mexican border. The large puddles in this photograph testify to the heavy rains that fell during this period of active duty.

John W. Converse, the troop stable sergeant, donated this mobile field kitchen to the troop. This field kitchen was one of several items not usually allotted to National Guard soldiers. It was drawn by four horses or mules and provided hot meals to troopers in the field. The number of photographs of this kitchen that survive strongly suggest that it was either a highly unusual item or immensely popular with troops in the field.

One of the most important rules for a cavalryman was to take care of his horse before he took care of himself. Here a soldier eats his meal from a mess tin, after having strapped on his mount's feed bag. The horse and soldier appear to carry a full field load.

Troopers are shown here firing their Model 1903 Springfield rifles at Dona Anna, New Mexico. The first two days on the range were accompanied by torrential downpours. The third day, shown here, was clear and cold, necessitating that they wear overcoats and sweaters.

A lone horseman is shown here during the early days of the Mexican border service at Camp Stewart, Texas. The camp that would eventually cover several hundred acres appears sparse at this point. As rains gave way to colder temperatures, a shack replaced the mess tent shown at right.

Here is another view of the troop's arrival at Fort Bliss. The rail journey, which passed through Washington, D.C., St. Louis, and Kansas City, took four days. At the far left, another group of soldiers is visible. They are probably Troop G, 1st Pennsylvania Cavalry, which made the trip on the same train.

The troop stands ready for rifle inspection at Camp Stewart. This photograph was probably taken soon after the troop's arrival in Texas, as there is little evidence of the huge camp that would soon rise on this spot. Just visible in the background are the seven-by-seven-foot tents that three men shared. These tents were soon replaced by larger pyramidal tents.

A trooper shows off his well-groomed mount and equipment. The trooper is dressed in the regulation 1916 cavalry uniform, and the horse is tacked with a double-reined cavalry bridle and Model 1904 McClellan saddle, which was the standard issue cavalry saddle at the time. The saddle has covered wooden stirrups designed to protect the rider from brambles, with a flag bucket mounted, suggesting that this horse belongs to the troop guidon bearer.

Within a few months of its return from the Mexican border, the troop was called into federal service following the Unites States' declaration of war on Germany. Many troopers were experienced soldiers who also held college degrees and were therefore in high demand as officer candidates. One of these men was Harry Ingersoll, shown at the center of the photograph. Ingersoll took a commission and rose to command a company of the 313th Infantry, 79th Division, organized at Camp Meade, Maryland, in 1917.

At the time the 79th Division organized in 1917, many of the temporary buildings at Camp Meade were still unpainted. This trio of officers can be identified as troopers by its automobile, which has Pennsylvania license plates.

The first officers' training camp was held at Fort Niagara from May 15, 1917, to August 15, 1917. At the camp, 25 troopers were commissioned as captains, 16 as first lieutenants, and 15 as second lieutenants. Here the training company that bore the bulk of troopers takes part in a road march.

In 1936, western Pennsylvania was hit by one of the worst floods of the 20th century. Pittsburgh and Johnstown were especially hard-hit. On March 20, 1936, the governor of Pennsylvania ordered the troop into state service to restore order and prevent looting. The troopers shown here carry their issued .45 automatic pistols and truncheons.

In 1936, the troop restored order in the flood-stricken towns of Tarentum and Natrona, near Pittsburgh. The rising waters had overflowed sewers, creating a serious health problem. Although the troop performed its service without horses, many troopers continued to wear their spurs over their rubber boots.

Troopers here fill their army station wagon with gasoline while on flood duty near Pittsburgh. The troop left its horses in Philadelphia and traveled west in motorized vehicles—a mode of travel that was a harbinger of things to come.

In March 1936, the troop mustered into state service to provide relief to flood-stricken towns in western Pennsylvania. Shown here are four of the six army one-and-a-half-ton trucks. At far left, an army station wagon, one of three used by the troop, is just visible. Troopers also drove three private automobiles during their stint of state service.

This image graphically shows the level of flood damage caused by the 1936 flood. Troopers are shown here guarding a street corner in one of the hard-hit areas. The troop patrolled these areas from March 23, 1936, until March 27, 1936.

The troop is shown here during the 1941 Carolina maneuvers. A line of picketed cavalry horses stands to the right. In the distance are pyramidal army tents. In the far distance are army trailer trucks used to transport horses and equipment. The soldiers are dressed in fatigue uniforms as they establish base camp.

Another view of the 1941 Carolina maneuvers shows the base camp in a little better order, with troopers tending to saddles and other horse equipment. This photograph was probably taken near Wadesboro, North Carolina, where the troop set up its base camp for three months.

A trooper cleans his .45-caliber automatic pistol during the 1941 Carolina maneuvers. He wears tall regulation cavalry boots and issue cavalry breeches. At right, his saddlebag awaits his attention.

A more extensive view of the troop's base camp at Wadesboro is visible here. This temporary camp consisted entirely of tents. At center, unsaddled horses stand in a picket line. While on maneuver, the troop usually spent its weekends here and slept in the field during the week.

In February 1941, the troop entered federal service as Troop A, 104th Cavalry Regiment (Horse Mechanized). Horse-mechanized regiments were an advanced concept in 1941. Tractor trailers would carry horses as far as the roads would take them to forward battle areas. Upon arrival, the regiment was to saddle up and fight on horseback. The troop is shown here during the Carolina maneuvers unloading a horse from a tractor trailer.

Another aspect of the horse-mechanized regiment was the machine gun platoon attached to each troop. Here members of the troop's machine gun platoon mount boxes filled with machine gun ammunition on a horse at Fort Indiantown Gap.

The machine gun platoon gets ready to ride out at Fort Indiantown Gap. Each machine gun trooper had two horses under his care. One of these horses served as his mount, the other carried his equipment. For this reason, members of the troop's machine gun platoon were a tightly knit group, as they normally had twice the daily chores of other soldiers. Tradition holds that machine gun troopers prided themselves on always being the first at everything and were usually the first soldiers to fall in for morning formation.

A member of the machine gun platoon prepares to fire a Model 1919 .30 Browning machine gun. The sandbags provided an extra rest for target work on the machine gun range. The machine gun, its ammunition, and its tripod mount were all carried on horseback by machine gun troopers, who were also responsible for their maintenance.

Two different views of the machine gun platoon during the last of the horse cavalry show troopers wearing Model 1917 steel helmets and web belts containing ammunition pouches for their Model 1903 Springfield rifles. The rifles were carried in saddle scabbards, one of which hangs to the right of the soldiers in the photograph below. In addition to rifles, troopers of the heavily armed machine gun platoon carried .45-caliber automatic pistols in holsters on their canvas web belts.

A soldier shows off his saddle and tack during the 1941 maneuvers in North Carolina. These maneuvers were the last time that the troop conducted extensive training on horseback and one of the last times that the troop trained together during World War II. Many troopers had departed or would soon depart to take officers' commissions in the army, navy, and marines.

Troopers rush out to mount their horses during training at Fort Indiantown Gap. Fort Indiantown Gap was a temporary army mobilization station mostly constructed in 1941. Many of its buildings still stand and have been used by the troop from the time of their construction up to the present day.

One of the first steps in grooming a horse is the picking of its hooves to prevent injury to the animal. Here a trooper performs this important function during prewar training. The device on the trooper's campaign hat is the First City Troop's insignia, first adopted in 1775. The presence of the device on the trooper's hat identifies him as a member of Headquarters Troop, 52nd Cavalry Brigade, and dates the photograph prior to September 22, 1940, when the troop reorganized as Troop A, 104th Cavalry Regiment (Horse Mechanized).

The troop reorganized as Troop A, 104th Cavalry Regiment (Horse Mechanized), on September 22, 1940. The circular brass device identifies this trooper as a member of that regiment. This trooper has loosened the distinctive chin strap worn by cavalrymen to help keep their broad-brimmed campaign hats on when riding on horseback, perhaps to enjoy the pleasure of the cigarette clenched resolutely in his teeth.

The temporary buildings of Fort Indiantown Gap were still in use in the early 1950s when this photograph was taken. Many had since been painted and, like this one, were now in need of another paint job. The troop is shown here standing in formation. The troop had long since ceased to train on horseback but continued to fill the important cavalry reconnaissance mission.

The needs of the army during the Korean War called for troops confronting the Soviet Union in Germany to redeploy to east Asia. As a result, the troop, along with the 28th Infantry Division, entered active federal service in 1951. Here troopers belly up to a field mess.

After completing training at Camp Atterbury and conducting maneuvers at Fort Bragg, North Carolina, the troop deployed to Germany with the rest of the 28th Infantry Division. Here a rifle squad from the troop has stopped its half-track along a road in Germany for a quick photograph.

The tank section of the 28th Mechanized Reconnaissance Troop stops on a snowy road in Germany. The troop tank section consisted at this time of two M-24 light tanks. In addition to the tank and rifle sections, the 28th Mechanized Reconnaissance Troop consisted of a mortar section and a headquarters platoon.

Another tank used by the troop in the 1950s was the M-41 Walker Bulldog medium tank. Troopers are shown here at the motor pool of Fort Indiantown Gap inspecting one of the newly arrived tanks. National Guard soldiers in state service were usually equipped with less-current equipment than the regular army.

A trooper gets ready to board a train when departing for active federal service during the Korean War in 1951. He wears the red keystone-shaped patch of the 28th Infantry Division. The chevrons identify him as a corporal, or junior noncommissioned officer. He wears a helmet liner made of nonmetal composite materials that is also decorated with a 28th Infantry Division keystone and his corporal's rank.

After entering federal service, the troop mobilized at Camp Atterbury and then participated in maneuvers at Fort Bragg, North Carolina. Here three troopers ride in a jeep alongside two tanks, which most likely carry their fellow troopers in the tank section.

Since 1942, the troop has been a mechanized cavalry unit, and troopers have been well acquainted with the many types of tank used by the U.S. Army. One of the timeless occupational hazards encountered by tankers is to be stuck in the mud. Such incidents usually draw the attention of non-tankers. A reluctant M-4 Sherman tanker poses for a photograph while a crew member digs out the tank and several unmuddied observers look on.

A group of 28th Reconnaissance troopers stands on the deck of the troopship USWS *General C. H. Muir*. The troop left Staten Island, New York, on November 16, 1951, and arrived at Bremerhaven, Germany, on November 28, 1951. Despite crowded conditions, the oceanic voyage was relatively calm.

Troopers conduct maneuvers during annual training in the late 1960s. The troop was at the time equipped with gun jeeps, visible in the rear, as well as tanks. The troopers in the foreground carry M-1 Garand rifles, which had gone out of service in the regular army but were still in use by reserve and National Guard soldiers.

A troop tank supports two cavalry scouts during training in the late 1960s. Armored-cavalry doctrine at the time called for lightly armed but highly mobile scouts to reconnoiter a battlefield. Should they encounter a superior enemy force, they could rely on the firepower of tanks working in close consort.

Troop officers in a jeep pose with members of a scout or rifle section during training in the late 1960s. The driver was usually a lower-ranking enlisted man who was also responsible for maintaining the vehicle.

Members of a troop scout or rifle section dismount from an M-113 armored personnel carrier. The troop trained with the reliable M-113 until recent years. This lightly armored vehicle was designed to carry a rifle squad over any terrain, including water.

Troopers are here shown using the versatile M-113 in another role, that of improvised command post. A squad studies a map or other training aid while in the field. Soldiers would virtually live aboard these tracked vehicles when in the field during annual training.

Troopers are here shown at the National Training Center at Fort Irwin, California, in 2001. The National Training Center provides rigorous and realistic training to soldiers in a desert environment. The troopers here wear the desert camouflage uniform. The white cloth material at their feet is known as engineer tape, used to mark off areas of terrain.

The troop was deployed to Bosnia and Herzegovina in 2002 to serve as peacekeepers enforcing the Dayton Peace Accords. Here a troop patrol rolls past a bullet-riddled house in one of its areas of responsibility. Such scenes were commonplace during this seven-month deployment.

A troop patrol stops for refreshment in a predominantly Muslim area of Bosnia and Herzegovina. A minaret stands among typical Bosnian houses, most of which appear to have been repaired since the war. The troopers enjoy beverages and sweets donated by two prominent Philadelphia food companies.

Troopers conduct urban training at Fort Indiantown Gap sometime in the early 21st century. The troop continues to train on this same ground as it has for over 60 years. In the distance is the geographic feature that gives Indiantown Gap its name.

A trooper uses his binoculars while on a mounted patrol in Bosnia and Herzegovina in late 2002. The primary mission of the troop was to provide mounted patrols in support of local authorities, as well as to enforce international peace accords and encourage Bosnians to turn in weapons used during the 1992–1995 civil war. Basic reconnaissance was a daily activity as the troop provided the eyes and ears of its higher headquarters. In this way, the troop's mission has changed very little in over 230 years of service to the nation.

Two

Armories
and Artifacts

On September 16, 1775, Capt. Abraham Markoe paid John Folwell £1.15 to design the troop's standard and at a later date paid James Claypoole £8 to paint a device, union, and motto. John Donnaldson noted that the figures in the standard are "a female with wings, blowing a trumpet held by the right hand & by the left a wand representing Fame. On the left the figure of an Indian warrior with bow & arrow & a pole with cap of Liberty d'or." Donnaldson noted that "the shield is mounted with a crest, a horse's head on which are worked in silver the letters LH—under the shield is the motto—For these we strive." The canton of 13 alternating stripes replaced an earlier Union Jack, a reminder that at the time of the standard's manufacture, the colonies had not yet declared independence. The troop has carried this standard or a copy in all its campaigns up to the present day.

One of the earliest images of the troop uniform is this one executed in 1823. This is the uniform worn when the troop escorted the Marquis de Lafayette during his visit to Philadelphia one year later. The red sash worn around the trooper's waist was not ordinarily a part of the troop's uniform; it nevertheless formed a part of the troop uniform until 1872.

The troop's first sergeant is here shown in the troop's fatigue uniform. The troop authorized this uniform to save wear and tear on the dress uniform when drilling or performing other duties. The first sergeant wears the flat-topped fatigue cap and red sash that were discontinued in 1872.

Troop officers are shown here sitting at the head table of a formal dinner at the troop's second armory during the late 19th century. Just visible behind the officers is the original Markoe standard. At the extreme right of the picture, the French tricolor carried by the troop when it escorted the Marquis de Lafayette in 1824 is visible. This tricolor is still in the troop's possession.

Capt. Joseph Lapsley Wilson stands in front of a vault containing the troop's first standard, bylaws, and muster roll. These artifacts, still in the troop's possession, are some of its earliest and most precious relics. Probably taken during Wilson's tenure as troop captain, which lasted between 1889 and 1894, Wilson is wearing the troop's ceremonial uniform. The satchel hanging on his left side is a sabretache, once used for carrying dispatches.

The troop is shown here celebrating an important anniversary at its second armory at Twenty-first and Ash Streets. The cased rifles in the background stand in sharp contrast to the table dressings and elaborate uniforms and serve as a reminder that the troop has always placed equal emphasis on military preparedness. This armory no longer stands. Following a severe snowstorm, which started on February 11, 1899, and continued for 48 hours, the roof of the troop's second armory collapsed. The damage was severe enough that the troop voted to build its third armory, the present home of the troop since 1901.

The troop has long been the subject of many works of art by various artists. Some of these renderings show the troop in a flattering light, others show the troop in a more humorous light. The caricature at right shows a trooper in full-dress uniform on his horse, as does the Frederic Remington image below. Both images are reasonably accurate depictions of the troop's full-dress uniform and horse equipment. The red covering under the saddle, known as a chevraque, and the white goatskin padding over the saddle were to be a part of the authorized equipment.

MOUNTED TROOPER, FIRST TROOP PHILADELPHIA CITY CAVALRY, BY FREDERIC REMINGTON

The troop trumpeter has always been a highly skilled as well as musically talented member of the unit. During the early years of the troop, the captain entrusted the trumpeter with important messages and notices to distribute to troopers at home. The trumpeter would then put on his uniform, mount his horse, and ride to the house of every trooper with the latest orders from the captain. The troop discontinued this practice as technology improved but continues the tradition of the trumpeter's messenger role by using his image on letterheads and other important correspondence.

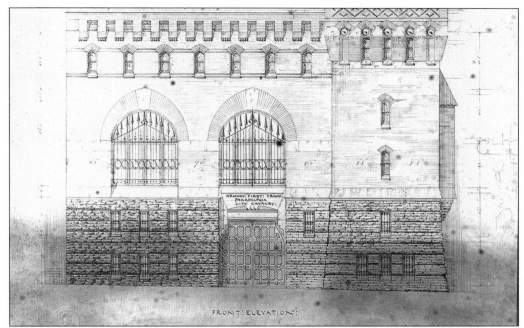

Noted Philadelphia architect Frank Furness designed the troop's second home, located at Twenty-first and Ash Streets (no longer extant) in Philadelphia. Furness had served with the 6th Pennsylvania Cavalry during the Civil War. At the Battle of Trevelyan station in 1864, Furness, while under fire, carried a crate of ammunition on his head to needy comrades, a feat for which he later earned the Medal of Honor.

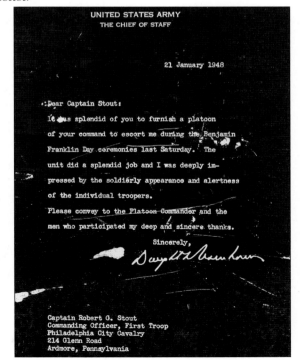

UNITED STATES ARMY
THE CHIEF OF STAFF

21 January 1948

Dear Captain Stout:

It was splendid of you to furnish a platoon of your command to escort me during the Benjamin Franklin Day ceremonies last Saturday. The unit did a splendid job and I was deeply impressed by the soldierly appearance and alertness of the individual troopers.

Please convey to the Platoon Commander and the men who participated my deep and sincere thanks.

Sincerely,

Dwight D. Eisenhower

Captain Robert G. Stout
Commanding Officer, First Troop
Philadelphia City Cavalry
214 Glenn Road
Ardmore, Pennsylvania

Throughout its history, the troop has had the honor to escort many important individuals. Among its many archives are letters of thanks from some of those for whom it has provided this service. In 1948, Gen. Dwight D. Eisenhower thanked Capt. R. Gwynne Stout for providing an escort platoon during his visit to Philadelphia.

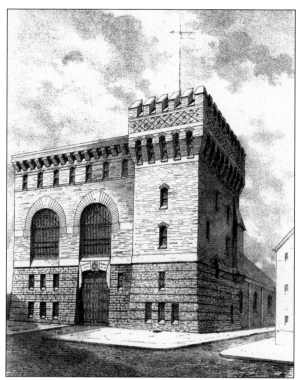

The troop's second armory stood at Twenty-first and Ash Streets and is seen here as it looked when dedicated in 1874. The Frank Furness–designed armory was used by the troop as a meeting place between 1874 and 1899. The large front doors opened onto an indoor training ring where the troop could conduct mounted drills year-round.

The troop's current armory was designed with all the latest amenities to provide the troop with an adequate training facility that could also serve as a barracks during emergencies. Heavily renovated over the last century, the troop continues to use the kitchen for its many dinners and celebrations, not to mention to fill the mouths of the many hungry soldiers who continue to drill there.

A troop inspection takes place sometime in the first half of the 20th century. The central area of the armory, known as the ring, was originally a wooden floor covered with dirt and used for the purpose of drilling on horseback. After World War II, the troop resurfaced the ring with asphalt to facilitate parking tanks, trucks, and jeeps.

The troop helmet continues to be one of the most distinctive articles of the troop's full-dress uniform. The body of the helmet is made of leather and is trimmed with white metal and topped with a bearskin roach. White metal laurel branches reminiscent of a crown decorate the sides. At the front of the helmet is an eagle device, and metal scales cover the chin strap.

The troop is one of the few units of its size authorized to carry more than one flag. In addition to the red and white cavalry guidon, the troop also carries the Markoe standard wherever it goes. Possibly one of its most important living artifacts, the Markoe standard and its device have been used as military insignia and artistic motif in numerous renderings. Two troopers are shown here riding on the back of a Humvee at the National Training Center at Fort Irwin, California, in 2001.

A trooper removes the troop's red and white "First Troop PCC" guidon while at Camp Stewart, Texas, in 1916. He replaces it with a guidon, but one reflecting the troop's service with the 1st Pennsylvania Cavalry. The troop was officially redesignated as Troop E, 1st Pennsylvania Cavalry, during the Mexican border service. The troop guidon, with its distinctive lettering, has been carried by the troop as an individual unit designator since at least the mid-19th century, when such flags came into general use. Like the Markoe standard, the troop can often be seen either marching or riding behind this distinctive flag.

The troop guidon is seen here during training at Fort Indiantown Gap during the mid-1970s. The silver rings around the guidon staff represent the many campaigns in which the troop has served since the Revolutionary War. As the troop continues to serve in new campaigns, these honors will undoubtedly grow. But since cloth streamers have recently replaced metal bands on unit guidons, these silver bands may soon become yet another part of the troop's extensive historical property on view at its museum in Philadelphia.

Three

CELEBRATING CITY LIFE

Presidential escorts have always been an important part of the pageantry that is the First City Troop, starting with George Washington in 1789. The troop escorted Pres. Woodrow Wilson on three separate occasions. On October 25, 1913, the troop escorted Wilson during a visit to Congress Hall. The following year, he returned to Philadelphia for Independence Day celebrations. In 1915, Wilson returned to Philadelphia, where he addressed newly naturalized citizens at Convention Hall in Fairmount Park. He is shown here accepting the American flag from a troop officer during this third visit.

The Philadelphia Light Horse performed its first active military service in June 1775, when it escorted Gen. George Washington as he left Philadelphia to take command of the newly organized Continental army at Boston. The 1775 troop escorted Washington only as far as New York, where it was relieved by a contingent of New York militia. In the spirit of the bicentennial celebration, the 1975 troop rode all the way to Boston, stopping at some point to enjoy a cruise on Pete Seeger's sloop *Clearwater*. They were photographed without the short brown coat that was the regulation uniform of the Philadelphia Light Horse in 1775.

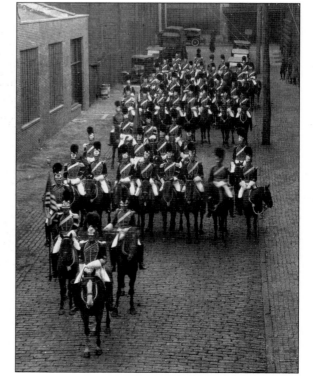

The troop here assembles in three platoons in preparation for one of its many parades. The guidon, in this case a swallow-tailed American flag, is carried at the head of the procession. A color-bearer carries the Markoe standard between the first and second platoons. Although taken in the 1920s, this scene has been repeated at least three times a year since the troop moved into this armory in 1901.

The troop parades through the city three times a year to commemorate its anniversary, Washington's birthday, and the memorial of Washington's death. These parades are always conducted in the full-dress uniform and never fail to attract a large crowd. On other occasions, the troop sallies forth to escort an important dignitary. Here the troop's color guard has ridden out the front door of the armory onto Twenty-third Street. Four troop riders abreast comprise the color guard. One rider carries the national color on the right, and one carries the Markoe standard on the left. Two other troopers ride with sabers drawn as guards. In this photograph, the riders have only just departed the armory and have not yet drawn their sabers. The color guard is one of the most important duties in a mounted escort.

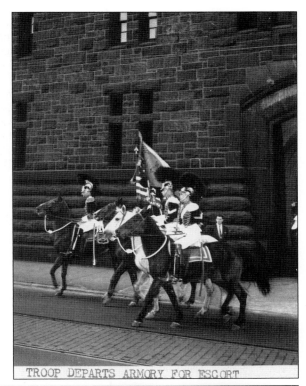

TROOP DEPARTS ARMORY FOR ESCORT

Capt. John C. Groome Sr. here rides in an open coach with Pres. Theodore Roosevelt, who doffs his hat to passersby. The troop escorted Roosevelt on three separate occasions. On November 22, 1902, the troop escorted Roosevelt on his visit to dedicate Central High School in Philadelphia, to the Union League on Broad Street, and to the residence of financier Edward T. Stotesbury on Rittenhouse Square. On January 30, 1905, the troop again escorted Roosevelt during his visit to the Union League. One month later, Roosevelt enjoyed the hospitality of the troop at what was then its new armory at Twenty-third and Ranstead Streets.

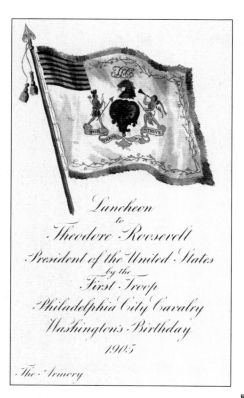

Luncheon
to
Theodore Roosevelt
President of the United States
by the
First Troop
Philadelphia City Cavalry
Washington's Birthday
1905

The Armory

On his third visit with the troop, Pres. Theodore Roosevelt attended a luncheon at the armory at which he thanked the troop for its service to the nation and maintaining its history and traditions. This lunch was only the second time that the troop had entertained a president as its guest. The first time had been on September 14, 1787, when Gen. George Washington visited the troop for dinner. Roosevelt's visit to the armory was in fact a first, as the 1787 dinner had been held before Washington's presidency.

At the time of the Spanish-American War, H. Engelmann's "First City Troop March and Two-Step" had been known to two generations of troopers. Upon the troop's return from the Spanish-American War, trumpeter Ellis Pugh had played the tune from the deck of a tug in New York Harbor. The cover image shows a band in its approximation of the troop uniform. The Union League on Broad Street stands as a backdrop.

On January 20, 1959, 38 troopers escorted Pennsylvania governor David Leo Lawrence at his inaugural ball at the Zembo Mosque in Harrisburg. The captain escorted the new governor past a receiving line of troopers. Lawrence, a former mayor of Pittsburgh, was the last Pennsylvania governor born in the 19th century and the first Roman Catholic governor of Pennsylvania. The troop wore the full-dress dismounted uniform, which consists of black leather shoes and light blue trousers with two red stripes running up the outside seam. All other uniform parts are the same as the mounted uniform.

The troop rides past the Real Estate Title Insurance and Trust Company during a Fourth of July celebration. Even today, parades like this often draw large crowds that stop traffic for many blocks in either direction.

On April 23, 1923, 48 veterans of the Spanish-American War troop held a reunion in Philadelphia. Seated in the second row, fifth from the right, is Capt. John C. Groome Sr. At the time this photograph was taken, Groome was the warden of Eastern State Penitentiary in Philadelphia. To his right is Capt. J. Franklin McFadden (fourth from left). Both officers wear the troop mess uniform, worn on formal occasions such as this.

The troop plays polo while serving near the Mexican border near Fort Bliss, Texas, at the end of 1916. Polo became a very popular sport with the troop on the Mexican border. Stable sergeant John W. Converse organized a polo league that practiced every day. In December, a four-man team representing the 1st Pennsylvania Cavalry, of which the troop was a part, beat the 17th Cavalry Regiment team in a match. This team, captained by Converse, consisted of troopers Wister Randolph, Barclay McFadden, Harry Ingersoll, and Hoxie Harrison Smith. This team also played Gen. John James Pershing's team in Mexico.

The troop celebrated its sesquicentennial in November 1924. The wives of eight troop officers who served as hostesses and received the guests at the troop sesquicentennial ball are shown here with their husbands. Effingham B. Morris, shown fourth from the left, wears no decorations, despite having been wounded in the same battle that took the life of his friend Harry Ingersoll during World War I. Capt. J. Franklin McFadden and Capt. John C. Groome Sr., standing second and third from the right, respectively, wear red sashes over their right shoulders. The red sashes indicate that they are no longer in active service.

Noncommissioned officers of the troop pose during the troop's sesquicentennial celebration. Noncommissioned officers are distinguished by chevrons on their sleeves and the white epaulets on their shoulders. Behind them is the bandstand set up for the three-day celebration.

Troop weddings are always special events. Here a troop wedding party treats a newlywed couple to the traditional ceremony of arched sabers. This old cavalry tradition is frequently performed at troop weddings. An American flag and the Markoe standard stand behind the couple.

Led by two trumpeters, the troop rides down Chestnut Street during its October 25, 1913, escort of Pres. Woodrow Wilson. Wilson visited Philadelphia on this occasion to attend festivities at Congress Hall, located next to Independence Hall. Riders had to be careful to ensure that their horses did not lose their footing on the steel trolley tracks.

Indoor Horse Polo
—AT—
THE NEW ARMORY
Thirty-Second St.—West Phila.
Saturday Afternoon, JAN. 22, at 2.30 O'clock

UNIVERSITY OF PENNSYLVANIA		BRYN MAWR POLO CLUB
versus	and	versus
FIRST CITY TROOP CAVALRY		PENLLYN POLO CLUB

LADIES' AND GENTLEMEN'S JUMPING CONTEST
BAND SELECTIONS

Admission - - - - $1.10
Including War Tax

Tickets on Sale at { A. G. SPAULDING & BROS., 1210 Chestnut Street
MARTIN & MARTIN, 1713 Chestnut St.
BRYN MAWR RIDING ACADEMY,
Morris Avenue, Bryn Mawr

The first polo match ever played by a troop team was at the Philadelphia Country Club grounds at Bala on May 23, 1896. On June 27, the troop won a polo match against the 6th U.S. Cavalry at Washington, D.C., in the first recognized polo match in the U.S. Army. The troop later organized a polo team while in federal service on the Mexican border. This notice announces a match between the University of Pennsylvania team and the troop to be held at the 103rd Cavalry Regiment armory at the corner of Thirty-second Street and Lancaster Avenue. The armory still stands and today houses the 103rd Engineer Battalion.

The troop prepares for a parade on the Benjamin Franklin Parkway around the time of its opening. The Philadelphia Museum of Art can just be seen in the background. The trooper who is mounted on the horse second from the left carries another version of the troop guidon, a swallow-tailed American flag.

A platoon of troopers marches down a street in formation. The troop rarely paraded outside the city, but records suggest that this may have been a parade through Harrisburg.

The troop marches past a reviewing stand on Broad Street in 1908. The newly built Forrest Theater is just to the left of center. The tall building behind it is the North American Building. To the far left is Philadelphia's city hall.

The troop rides down Market Street during a parade near the beginning of the 20th century. The troop is formed in two platoons with an officer at the head of each platoon. Helmeted Philadelphia police officers maintain crowd control. The troop was not the only military organization in the city; another unit marches some distance behind.

By February 22, 1919, many troopers were still in France. Sixty-one members held a dinner at the armory in Philadelphia, while others celebrated Washington's birthday in France. The French dinner featured oysters and endive salad. The troop traditionally celebrates its important anniversaries wherever the needs of the service may find it.

The troop is shown here presenting sabers to Pennsylvania governor David Leo Lawrence at his inaugural ball held in Harrisburg in 1959. The presentation of sabers is a military courtesy rendered of salute. The officers on the right hold their sabers to the side as a means of saluting the Pennsylvania chief executive.

Since its earliest days, strong family ties have always bound the troop. Boys frequently follow their older brothers, fathers, and uncles into the organization. Here a troop corporal has dressed his young son in a troop uniform. The adult trooper wears a flat-topped fatigue of pillbox hat with his full-dress mounted uniform.

Upon its return from Puerto Rico, the troop pulled into the train station at Broad and Washington Streets. There mounted on horses supplied by the Philadelphia Police Department, the troop rode to Horticultural Hall, where a banquet awaited. Along the way, cannons saluted them from the roof of the Union League and crowds cheered them. Some of the well-wishers shouted, "Here come the Rough Riders," as the troop rode past, mistaking the troop for Theodore Roosevelt's famous regiment.

The troop is shown here during its sesquicentennial ball, which began on the evening of November 15, 1924. Two-thirds of the armory floor, which consists of a practice ring for military drills and was at the time covered in dirt, was decked over with a dance floor. The ceiling and walls were covered with yellow and white cloth, and the 1774–1924 decoration lit with electric lights. A 40-piece orchestra accompanied the celebration, which lasted until 4:00 the next morning. Two more days of celebration followed.

During the third and final day of its sesquicentennial celebration in 1924, the troop rode to a reception held in its honor by Philadelphia mayor W. Freeland Kendrick. The troop here rides past the Second Bank of the United States at Fourth and Chestnut Streets. The bank's columns are just visible through the trees.

On April 6, 1924, the troop buried Capt. George Chapman Thayer with full military honors. The troop, along with detachments from each troop of the 1st Squadron, 103rd Cavalry, lined the aisles of the Church of the Redeemer in Haverford. The 1st Squadron of the 103rd Cavalry was Thayer's last command. Following the funeral, trumpeter emeritus Ellis Pugh played taps, and the troop's firing squad, shown here, fired three volleys over the grave.

Three troopers pose in full-dress mounted uniform. Their epaulets indicate that they are among the lowest-ranking members in the organization.

November 17, 1950   Lt William L. Hires house
                     in Nashville, Indiana

On June 25, 1950, North Korean tanks crashed across the 38th parallel into the Republic of Korea, and troops from Germany were needed as reinforcements there. So on September 5, 1950, the army ordered the troop into active federal service as the 28th Mechanized Reconnaissance Troop, part of Pennsylvania's 28th (Keystone) Infantry Division. The troop first traveled to Camp Atterbury, Indiana, for training. Despite its federal status, the troop continued to observe its old traditions. A contingent of troopers here celebrates the anniversary of the troop's organization on November 17, 1950.

The troop holds a monthly dinner sometime in the late 1960s. The inside of the troop armory has changed considerably over the years, but the basic decor has remained more or less constant. Old troop guidons are customarily displayed around the room. The guidon at the center of the photograph is not a French tricolor, it is an improvised guidon carried by the troop when in state service at Hazleton in 1897.

A contingent of troopers carries sabers during Fourth of July festivities at the state capitol in Harrisburg in 2003. This is a position of attention for cavalry soldiers under arms. Full-dress parades outside Philadelphia are relatively rare occurrences for the troop; however, the troop is ready to provide service to the commonwealth when asked. When called to do so, the troop is still quite capable of providing a timeless military flair to official events.

The troop celebrated its 142nd anniversary at the Hotel Paso del Norte in El Paso, Texas, on November 17, 1916, while in federal service. This was the first time the troop celebrated an anniversary while in federal service since the War of 1812. Quartermaster John Wagner provided turtles, a Philadelphia favorite, for the troopers' dinner. Early the next morning, the troop was back at work, holding an equipment inspection at Camp Stewart.

The captain leads the troop in a column of fours down a Philadelphia street. Between 1925 and 1926, the troop took part in many full-dress mounted parades. On November 10, 1925, the troop turned out in full-dress mounted order to participate in the 150th anniversary of the founding of the Marine Corps. On June 2, 1926, the troop escorted the crown prince and princess of Sweden from Logan Square to Independence Hall and Old Swedes' Church. On June 14 and 15, 1926, the troop participated in formal dedication ceremonies for the city's sesquicentennial celebration. Three days later, a detachment escorted Secretary of the Treasury Andrew Mellon for the dedication of the Robert Morris statue on the steps of the Second Bank of the United States.

Fairman Rogers

On March 4, 1872, "upon the approach of the Centennial Anniversary of the formation of the Troop," the troop organized a committee headed by Fairman Rogers and consisting of William Camac, M. Edward Rogers, Archibald Loudon Snowden, Joseph R. Wilkins Jr., James J. McDowell, Joseph Lapsley Wilson, and William D. Gemmill to write the first published history of the troop. No comprehensive history had been compiled since the appearance of John Donnaldson's narrative almost 50 years earlier. The troop had performed a great many deeds in the intervening years.

Four

A LIVING LEGACY

Well educated and worldly, Princeton University graduate John R. C. Smith sailed all over the world as a representative of the firm of Willing and Francis before becoming captain of the troop in 1817. The first captain born after the American Revolution, Smith wrote in 1823 that "the Troop is identified with the revolutionary history of our country & was at all times conspicuously useful in the arduous struggle to establish our Liberty & Rights." Smith was probably the first captain to systematically compile the troop's historical records. In October 1823, Smith approached John Donnaldson, one of seven surviving Revolutionary War troopers, and asked him to compile one of the earliest surviving accounts of the troop's service during the Revolutionary War. This image is from a portrait by Thomas Sully.

John C. Groome Jr., the son of Capt. John C. Groome Sr., enlisted with the troop in 1916 and served therein on the Mexican border. He served as an officer in both world wars and as captain of the troop before leaving the army as a lieutenant colonel in 1943. This caricature shows him in 1917 when he was first sergeant of the troop, the highest-ranking enlisted man in the organization.

Born a Danish subject about 1733, Abraham Markoe immigrated to Philadelphia as a young man. As its first captain, Markoe helped organize and ready the Philadelphia Light Horse for war. Under his captaincy, the troop escorted Gen. George Washington to New York in the summer of 1775. In early 1776, when King Christian VII of Denmark issued an edict that any Danish subject in arms against George III of England would have his property confiscated, Markoe resigned. Markoe nevertheless remained a valuable supporter in the struggle for independence, and there is evidence that he fought on the American side at the Battle of Brandywine, although it is unlikely that he did so as a member of the Philadelphia Light Horse.

On May 17, 1917, Capt. J. Franklin McFadden resigned from the troop. In the course of 30 years of service with the troop, McFadden rose from the rank of private to commanding officer, served as an officer during the Spanish-American War, and commanded the troop on the Mexican border. His military service did not end with his resignation from the troop. He is shown here as a major and later lieutenant colonel in France, where among other duties he was responsible for German prisoners of war. (U.S. Army photograph.)

Cooper Howell joined the troop on April 3, 1911. He was promoted to corporal on December 15, 1915. On January 3, 1916, the troop appointed him as its historian. Howell served with the troop during the Mexican border service from 1916 to 1917. On May 26, 1917, Howell was commissioned a second lieutenant of cavalry. He attended the first officers' training course with other troopers at Fort Niagara in 1917. During World War I, he served with the 313th Infantry, 79th Division, and the 57th Field Artillery.

Harry Ingersoll enlisted in the First Troop Philadelphia City Cavalry, Pennsylvania Army National Guard, on October 7, 1912, and served with the troop on the Mexican border, where he was part of the regimental polo team. He was commissioned as a second lieutenant of cavalry on May 2, 1917. Shown here after he was promoted to captain, Ingersoll wears the insignia of Company H, 313th Infantry, 79th Infantry Division. During the first day of the Meuse-Argonne Offensive, September 27, 1918, Ingersoll led Company H in an assault on a German pillbox near Montfaucon. Cut down by machine gun fire, Ingersoll died several hours later.

The troop's first recorded encounter with Gen. John James Pershing occurred while in federal service on the Mexican border. Pershing was leading the United States' Punitive Expedition into Mexico and invited the polo team from the 1st Pennsylvania Cavalry to play his team. Polo was a serious sport in the premechanized cavalry, and tradition holds that the Philadelphians played their regular army counterparts to a draw. This early acquaintance grew into a cordial friendship. In 1922, Pershing attended a Washington's birthday luncheon at the troop's armory, accompanied by his aide, the future general George C. Marshall. Soon after, the troop made Pershing an honorary member at the armory, where he proudly poses in front of a tablet displaying troop captains wearing his troop honorary medal. As the general was not one to wear many decorations, this photograph speaks volumes of the pride with which he accepted this honor.

Capt. William Stokes sits in a chair that once belonged to Capt. Samuel Morris, the second captain of the troop. On the table next to Stokes is a silver tankard once owned by Morris. The corner cabinet behind Stokes contains his other uniforms. Stokes enlisted in the troop in December 1939 and served with the unit during maneuvers near Plattsburgh, New York, in 1940. Stokes shortly thereafter completed a correspondence course and was commissioned a second lieutenant of cavalry. Stokes served as commander of the 57th Cavalry Reconnaissance Troop on the Texas border between 1943 and 1946. Following the war, he reenlisted in the troop as a sergeant but by May 1948 was again an officer. Stokes led the troop to Germany in 1951. He retired as a brigadier general in the Pennsylvania National Guard in 1972.

All the living captains of the troop pose here in the late 1960s in front of a tablet bearing their names and dates of command. The captains all wear matching ties patterned in the troop colors, brown, gold, and white. These colors hearken back to the first troop uniform adopted at the beginning of the Revolutionary War, which was a brown coat trimmed and edged with white. The marble tablet still hangs in the front entrance of the armory. It has since been joined by a second identical tablet.

Trumpeter Joseph M. Harrison poses for the camera at the Radnor Hunt Club during the troop's annual equestrian competition known as the Border Plate. The Mexican border service also inaugurated an equestrian competition known as the Border Plate. This classic, which has run since 1922 and was only interrupted during wartime, showcases troopers' equestrian abilities. The competition takes its name in commemoration of the troop's Mexican border service and the first prize, which is a silver plate. Harrison's bugle is adorned with a yellow tabard embroidered with the troop's crest.

Capt. J. Franklin McFadden is shown here shaving in the field during the Mexican border service, probably at the Dona Anna rifle range, New Mexico, in October 1916. The troop's guidon lies rolled in the foreground along with items of McFadden's kit. The general disarray of the scene provides some indication that the unit was on the march at the time this photograph was taken.

October 1917 Camp Hancock Georgia

Volunteer instructor

At a stated meeting held on June 1, trumpeter Ellis Pugh wrote a letter stating that his present enlistment would expire and that owing to physical disability he would be disqualified from reenlisting in the National Guard. In consideration of his long and faithful service of 29 years as troop trumpeter and at the unanimous request of members present, Capt. John C. Groome Sr. appointed him trumpeter emeritus. In 1917, Pugh came out of retirement to train army musicians at Camp Hancock near Augusta, Georgia. He had first enlisted in the army in 1861.

During his 29 years with the First City Troop, John Dunlap rose from the rank of cornet, the lowest-ranking officer in the organization, to captain, a post to which the body elected him in 1794. In civilian life, the Irish-born Dunlap published the *Pennsylvania Packet or General Advertiser* and served as the official printer of the Continental Congress. In this capacity, he had the distinction of printing the first public copies of the Declaration of Independence. John Dunlap commanded the First City Troop when it mustered to put down the Whiskey Rebellion in 1794. This image is from a portrait by Rembrandt Peale.

Stable sergeant John Wagner poses in a folding camp chair with another trooper in this post-Spanish-American War carte de visite. This photograph was almost certainly taken shortly after the troop's return from Puerto Rico. Wearing their field uniforms and holding bottles of liquid refreshment, the two men exude the elation of homecoming soldiers. Upon its return from Puerto Rico, the City of Philadelphia feted the troop for days. At a banquet, well-wishers bestowed gifts commemorating the Spanish-American War service. Wagner stayed in the troop another two years before moving on.

John Borthwick enlisted as a private in the troop in April 1861 and served with the troop during its three months' service. On November 7, 1861, Borthwick was commissioned as an engineer in the U.S. Navy and is here shown wearing the uniform of that service.

Thomas C. James

Capt. Thomas C. James joined the troop on November 17, 1838, and was elected captain in 1850. He commanded the troop during its three months' service. When the troop mustered, the governor of Pennsylvania offered a commission as lieutenant colonel of the 9th Pennsylvania Cavalry, which he accepted. While stationed in Tennessee, James served as military governor of Clarksville and later chased roving Confederate cavalry in Kentucky. James was with the 9th Pennsylvania as it covered the retreat of the Union army following the Battle of Richmond. In October 1862, James was promoted to colonel and returned to Philadelphia in failing health. The former captain of the troop died on January 13, 1863.

An accomplished soldier, equestrian, and all-around athlete, Capt. J. Franklin McFadden attended the University of Pennsylvania, where he was a member of the varsity football team and tennis team. McFadden graduated in 1882 with a bachelor of science degree and went to work at the firm of his father, a cotton merchant and exporter. In 1887, McFadden joined the troop, where he participated in all the campaigns up to the Mexican border service. McFadden left the active troop but not the military in 1917. His service in France was distinguished. Here McFadden receives the French Legion of Honor from a high-ranking French officer. (U.S. Army photograph.)

Trumpeter Joseph M. Harrison here wears the uniform of a troop trumpeter. The colors of the trumpeter's uniform are the opposite of other troop uniforms in that the coat is red with blue trim. Harrison retired from the military on June 12, 1977, with 40 years, 10 months of service. A veteran of the prewar horse cavalry, Harrison served as a paratrooper in World War II. Here he wears his decorations, which include a Presidential Unit Citation, Bronze Star, and Purple Heart, among many others. Harrison served as troop trumpeter from 1948 to 1981. He accompanied the troop to Germany in 1951.

Trumpeter Ellis Pugh poses here during the Civil War. Although there is no record that Pugh served as a musician during the Civil War, this photograph taken by famed photographer Matthew Brady suggests otherwise.

1864 age 17 years

Another view of Ellis Pugh shows the future troop trumpeter in the uniform of a Union army private taken against an artificial backdrop upon which a camp scene has been painted. Pugh makes a show of loading his Enfield rifle musket.

Nicholas Sellers poses for a photograph in South Vietnam sometime in the late 1960s while serving as an advisor for the South Vietnamese army. Sellers joined the troop in 1953 and served with the unit for almost six years before taking a commission in the U.S. Army Reserve. He later served with both the U.S. Special Forces and the Republic of Vietnam Special Forces before retiring from the army as a colonel. In civilian life, Sellers was an assistant district attorney for Philadelphia for many years.

Ellis Pugh is shown here in his machine shop, the handwritten caption satirically commenting that he is here "working hard," in contrast to his dedication to the troop as its trumpeter. Another note points to a lithograph of the Battle of Gettysburg on the wall of his shop. Pugh had served in the Union army during the Civil War. Clearly his affinity for military minutia was not limited to his service with the First City Troop.

The five Cadwalader brothers are here shown at a summer encampment near Norristown in 1888 posing with some of the troop's weapons, including Model 1873 Winchester carbines that the troop carried between 1874 and 1898. All of them later served in the troop, one, Thomas Cadwalader, as the troop's captain.

John H. Hunter 2nd

John H. Hunter is shown here in the early 1930s, when he was a sergeant in the troop. Before joining the troop in 1923, Hunter served in the U.S. Army, first as a field artillery officer and later in the air service as an observer and gunner. On June 10, 1941, Hunter returned to the U.S. Army Air Forces and served in the China-Burma-India theater.

Capt. Joseph Lapsley Wilson is shown at left with his officers about 1894. The other officers are John C. Groome Sr. (second from right), Frank E. Patterson, and Edmund H. McCullough. Wilson's first military service was in 1862 with Company C, Gray Reserves, a Philadelphia Militia unit that spent several months on the Maryland border that year. Following the war, Wilson enlisted in the troop. John C. Groome Sr. joined the troop in 1882 and commanded the unit during the Spanish-American War. In civilian life, Groome founded the Pennsylvania State Police and served as the warden of Eastern State Penitentiary in the 1920s.

After serving with the troop during its three months' service in 1861, Horace Y. Evans was appointed as a surgeon in the U.S. Army in 1863. He served in that capacity throughout the war and died in 1908.

Hon. Henry H. Reed
Trooper 1098

Henry H. Reed was one of many troopers that Capt. J. Franklin McFadden encouraged to attend the officers' training course at Fort Niagara in 1917. Troop records show that Reed served as an officers' training course instructor and later as adjutant of the 305th Field Artillery in France. He wears the insignia and rank of a major in the 13th Cavalry Regiment.

Hon. LT. J. Willis Martin
Trooper 948

Sgt. J. Willis Martin joined the troop in 1889 and in 10 years rose to the rank of second lieutenant. Martin was the troop first sergeant during the Spanish-American War and left the active troop in 1904 to become judge in the court of common pleas in Philadelphia.

Hon. Crawford C. Madeira, Jr.
Trooper 1444

Capt. Crawford Clark Madeira served as the troop captain from 1933 to 1937. A 1916 graduate of the University of Pennsylvania, Madeira organized and headed the Benjamin Franklin Associates, a university fund group. Madeira joined the troop the same year he graduated from college and served with the troop for seven months on the Mexican border. He served with the 16th Cavalry in World War I and in various commands during World War II. Madeira was the vice president of different coal companies and a director of the National Coal Association.

Hon Lt. Frederic C. Wheeler
Trooper 1220

The troop has had many members who were associated with the Marine Corps both before and after they served with the troop. Perhaps the most famous trooper with a marine connection was William Ward Burrowes, who served four years with the troop before leaving its active ranks to become the first commandant of the Marine Corps in 1798. Frederic C. Wheeler is shown in the uniform of a troop officer, a rank he held between 1930 and 1937. Wheeler began his military service in the 10th Connecticut Field Artillery, a National Guard unit. In 1916, the Marine Corps commissioned Wheeler as a second lieutenant. During the course of World War I, Wheeler rose to the rank of captain. He does not wear the Bronze Star and Purple Heart he earned in combat.

124

Charles "Pete" Conrad Jr. served with the troop between 1949 and 1955. In 1955, Conrad graduated from the U.S. Navy's Pensacola Air Training Center with the highest honors. Conrad subsequently entered the space program. In November 1966, Capt. Thomas George Ashton dispatched a troop detachment to Harrisburg to escort Conrad, who had just returned from an eight-day space voyage. In 1969, Conrad was the third person to walk on the moon. On January 19, 1970, the troop provided an honor guard and escort for Conrad and the other Apollo 12 astronauts. (Right, U.S. Navy photograph; below, NASA photograph.)

CHARLES CONRAD, JR.

Troopers continue to carry on the centuries-old traditions of their organization. In 2005, six members of the troop deployed to Iraq. One of them was unable to make this photograph, but all returned in early 2006. The troop literally wears its history on its uniform; the first campaign credits earned by the troop at the Battles of Trenton and Princeton are embroidered on this sabretache. Troopers are acutely aware of their past but eagerly look to the challenges that lie ahead. (Photograph by John Bansemer.)

TROOP CAPTAINS

Abraham Markoe
Samuel Morris
Samuel Miles
Christian Febiger
John Dunlap
Robert Wharton
Charles Ross
John R. C. Smith
Lynford Lardner
William H. Hart
John Butler
Thomas C. James
Fairman Rogers
M. Edward Rogers
Archibald Loudon Snowden
Edward Burd Grubb
Joseph Lapsley Wilson
John C. Groome Sr.
J. Franklin McFadden
George Chapman Thayer
Thomas Cadwalader
Clement Biddle Wood
Effingham B. Morris Jr.
Crawford Clark Madeira
John C. Groome Jr.
Henry Brinton Coxe Jr.
Robert Norton Downs III
Robert Gwynne Stout
Robert Sturgis Ingersoll Jr.
William Standley Stokes Jr.
Henry P. Glendinning Jr.
Henry McKean Ingersoll
Thomas George Ashton
G. Jeremy Cummin

Murray Howard Dawson
Stanley Bright III
Alexander Kerr
Marcel Francois Lamour
Dennis J. Boylan
Simeon Dimitrivich Isayeff
Richard Drew Hughes
Keith Dagit Rogers
Christopher Smythe
Harry J. Gobora III
Eric E. L. Guenther Jr.
Lawrence J. Field
Anselm T. W. Richards

ACROSS AMERICA, PEOPLE ARE DISCOVERING SOMETHING WONDERFUL. *THEIR HERITAGE.*

Arcadia Publishing is the leading local history publisher in the United States. With more than 3,000 titles in print and hundreds of new titles released every year, Arcadia has extensive specialized experience chronicling the history of communities and celebrating America's hidden stories, bringing to life the people, places, and events from the past. To discover the history of other communities across the nation, please visit:

www.arcadiapublishing.com

Customized search tools allow you to find regional history books about the town where you grew up, the cities where your friends and family live, the town where your parents met, or even that retirement spot you've been dreaming about.

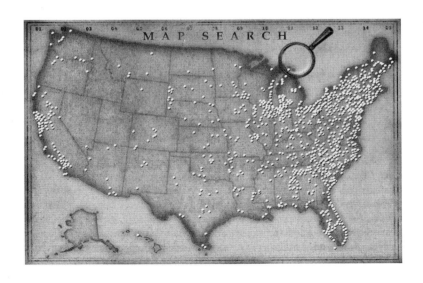